BACKYARD SAFARI

Owls

Wil Mara

Cavendish
Square

New York

Published in 2014 by Cavendish Square Publishing, LLC
303 Park Avenue South, Suite 1247, New York, NY 10010

Library of Congress Cataloging-in-Publication Data

Mara, Wil.
Owls / by Wil Mara.
p. cm. — (Backyard safari)
Includes index.
ISBN 978-1-62712-298-6 (hardcover) ISBN 978-1-62712-299-3 (paperback) ISBN 978-1-62712-300-6 (ebook)
1. Owls — Juvenile literature. I. Mara, Wil. II. Title.
QL696.S8 M28 2014
598.9'7—dc23

Editorial Director: Dean Miller
Senior Editor: Peter Mavrikis
Copy Editor: Cynthia Roby
Art Director: Jeffrey Talbot
Designer: Joseph Macri
Photo Researcher: Alison Morretta
Production Manager: Jennifer Ryder-Talbot
Production Editor: Andrew Coddington

The photographs in this book are used by permission and through the courtesy of: Cover photo by Mike Hill/age fotostock/Getty Images; Amy White & Al Petteway/National Geographic/Getty Images, 4; Lewis Phillips/Oxford Scientific/Getty Images, 5; Bruce Corbett/All Canada Photos/Getty Images, 6; Mark Newman/Lonely Planet Images/Getty Images, 8; Visuals Unlimited, Inc./Adam Jones/Visuals Unlimited/Getty Images, 9; NHPA / SuperStock, 10; Harold Wilion/Photolibrary/Getty Images, 11; Maslowski Steve/Photo Researchers/Getty Images, 13; Mark Hamblin/Oxford Scientific/Getty Images, 16; John Mitchell/Photo Researchers/Getty Images, 17; Cultura Limited / SuperStock, 20; Ambient Images Inc. / SuperStock, 22; E R DEGGINGER/Photo Researchers/Getty Images, 22; Richard Nowitz/National Geographic/Getty Images, 23; FLPA / SuperStock, 23; Piumatti Sergio / Prisma / SuperStock, 23; Joe McDonald/Visuals Unlimited/Getty Images, 23; imagebroker.net / SuperStock, 25; Gerard Lacz Images / SuperStock, 26.

Printed in the United States of America

Contents

Introduction 4

ONE An Owl's Life 5

TWO You Are the Explorer 13

THREE A Guide to Owls 21

FOUR Try This! Projects You Can Do 24

Glossary 29

Find Out More 30

Index 31

Introduction

Have you ever watched a squirrel chasing another squirrel around a tree? Or a group of deer leaping gracefully through a stretch of winter woods? If you have, then you know how wonderful it is to discover nature for yourself. Each book in the Backyard Safari series takes you step-by-step on an easy outdoor adventure, and then helps you identify the animals you've found. You'll also learn ways to attract, observe, and protect these valuable creatures. As you read, be on the lookout for the Safari Tips and Trek Talk facts sprinkled throughout the book. Ready? The fun starts just steps from your back door!

ONE
An Owl's Life

Owls are members of a family of animals called **Aves**, or birds. They have claws, feathers, beaks, and all that other good stuff that makes a bird a bird. Most adult owls are about 1 to 1.5 feet (0.3–0.5 m) in length, but they can be as small as 5 inches (13.5 cm) or as large as 32 inches (81 cm). An owl's "base" color can vary greatly, from dark brown or gray to a light gray or white. Within those base colors are a variety of other shades and tones. It is interesting to note that most owls will be colored

in a way that allows them to blend into their surroundings. For instance, white owls are commonly found in snowy areas, and brown owls are usually found in wooded areas. This natural **camouflage** makes it difficult for other animals to see them. This not only helps to protect owls from **predators** but also makes it easier for them to sneak up on their own **prey**.

Owls are usually colored in a way that helps them blend into their surroundings. This is called camouflage.

Owls have large, roundish heads. On their faces are two large, round eyes with circular pupils. Other night-dwelling creatures, such as cats, have slit-like pupils. Their eyes are one of their most important physical **characteristics** because they absorb a great deal of light. This permits an owl to see better during the night than many other creatures, including people! It is interesting to note that owls cannot move their eyes around in their sockets like we can. Instead, they have to move their entire heads. They have more **vertebrae** in their necks than we do, which allows them to turn their heads about three-quarters of the way around. We can't turn our heads more than about one quarter of the way around.

An owl's large pupils help them absorb as much light as possible, which gives them excellent night vision.

Trek Talk
Owls have incredible night vision—but only for long distances. Their eyes have evolved to enable them to spot movement by prey that are far away but not for movement that is close by. This means most owls are nearsighted! Anything that's too close to them appears blurry and is hard for them to identify.

Just as owls hunt by sight, they also hunt by sound. They have a few important physical features that help with this. On many owl **species**, the ears are not symmetrical—that is, they are not positioned in the same place on each side of its head. By being positioned differently, the ears are actually better at pinpointing the location of an animal they are trying to find. Their ears also have feathers that "trap" sounds, which make hearing easier. Many owls can further capture sounds with the aid of a **facial disc**, which is basically a circular arrangement of feathers that runs around their face. When a sound wave hits this disc, the sound is then directed to their ears.

Once an owl decides where its prey is located, it flies toward the animal with feathers that are designed to keep noise to a minimum. An

Many owl species have a circular feather array around their faces, which helps them to hear better.

owl's feathers are larger than those of most other birds. Their "flight feathers" have edges that are serrated—meaning they have little cuts all along the edges. They also have a soft quality that helps to quiet any noise made by each flap as it flies through the air. This is a very important feature because most prey animals know that they are prey for other animals. They are always on the alert for those that want to eat them! An owl that successfully reaches its prey then uses two other bodily features: very sharp **talons**, which are good for grabbing their prey, and then a small, downward-curved beak that, along with the talons, will help to lift and carry it away.

Owls also have voices. You may have heard that they "hoot." In fact, owls make a variety of sounds. They also screech, hiss, and even let out a kind of scream. They make different sounds for different reasons. Even owl experts aren't certain why owls make all the sounds that they do—the most common being to mark their territory and to warn others not to enter it. They also use sound as a warning signal and to locate other owls.

An owl's talons are very sharp. They make it easier to grab their prey off the ground.

Where They Live

Owls have established themselves all over the world. In fact, the only places that don't have at least one owl species are Antarctica and some small oceanic islands. They are remarkably hardy birds, meaning they can live under difficult conditions. This makes them able to live in a broad variety of **habitats**. You can find them in snow-covered ranges or dry deserts, in forests and grasslands, and even in areas heavily populated by people such as suburbs or cities. As long as they can find a place to rest during the day and plenty of food to hunt at night, they seem content.

Owls can fly with very little noise. This helps them to catch their prey without warning.

What They Do

Most owls live a solitary life, which means one owl basically lives by itself for most of the time. Owls are also **nocturnal**, meaning active at night. Some species are active during dawn and dusk, and a few come out during the day, but these are the exceptions to the rule. Once the sun goes down, their primary concern is feeding. Owls are among the most skilled hunters in the animal kingdom. They are **carnivorous**, which means they feed on other animals—as opposed to herbivores, which only eat plants. It's hard to say what their favorite food items are, as they can only eat what's available in their area. The most common animals preyed upon

If this owl made a lot of noise while flying, its prey—the mouse on the ground—would hear the noise and run off before the owl could catch it.

by owls include small **mammals** such as mice and voles, a variety of fish, other birds (although they rarely attack other owls for the purpose of feeding), some small reptiles and amphibians, and even **invertebrates** like worms, spiders, crabs, and certain insects. But don't be concerned as you head out on your safari—they don't eat people!

The Cycle of Life

Owls can mate at different times of the year, but most commonly in the spring. This is certainly the case in places that have both warm and cold seasons. Owl mothers will lay about four or five eggs, although as few as one and as many as a dozen is not unusual. In a few owl species, males and females stay together as a pair throughout a breeding season. In other species, males and females will stay together for life. Owls are very **territorial** by nature. They protect the area in which they live and don't like other owls invading it. This is most obvious during breeding season. Owls vigorously protect their nesting sites—violently if necessary. They will watch their hatchlings closely and make sure they are well fed. The males usually provide the food while the females stay with the young, which are usually called owlets or fledglings. It can take anywhere from three to ten weeks before the babies begin flying on their own, depending on the species. It can also take another month or so before they fly off to find their own homes. Most owls live about five to seven years, but some species can live up to eighteen or twenty.

TWO

You Are the Explorer

As you now know, owls are most active during the night. This can make it challenging to see them—but not impossible. There are bird enthusiasts, or people interested in birds, all over the world who go "owl watching" all the time. Owls are among the most interesting animals to see. This is not only for their remarkable hunting skills but also for their majestic beauty. Read over the tips given here to make your owl safari as successful and productive as possible.

Binoculars are a must-have item when you go on an owl safari.

What Do I Wear?

　❋　Old clothes that can get dirty.
　❋　Clothes that are loose-fitting and, most impotantly, comfortable.
　❋　Clothes that are dark in color. Brightly colored clothes may distract both the owls and their prey, which won't help you on your safari!
　❋　Any type of shoes will do, but those with soft soles are probably best.
　❋　Bug spray

What Do I Take?

　❋　Binoculars. Those with "night-vision" are best, but these can be expensive. Still, if you can get a pair, do so—they're perfect for owl safaris.
　❋　Flashlight (to be used only when necessary—more details to come).
　❋　Digital camera
　❋　Notebook
　❋　Cell phone

　❋　Pen or pencil
　❋　A folding chair
　❋　A snack for yourself

Where Do I Go?

Owls don't have a huge home range, that is, the area in which they live. If you already know of an area where owls can be found, then that's where you should be. If you don't already have this information, check the Internet to find ideal "owl spots" near your home. Since owls are such widespread creatures, there's a very good chance you'll be able to locate some within a reasonable distance.

❋ Wooded areas. Most owls love trees. They will sleep on branches or in tree holes during the day. They'll sit in these spots during the night while waiting for prey to appear. The absolute best trees are those in a group with other trees and have plenty of cover. This means big leaves, vine tangles, and other overgrowth that helps them to remain hidden.

❋ Near bodies of water such as streams, rivers, lakes, or ponds. This is where many of their prey animals will be found. If that's where they are, then that's where the owls will hunt. Remember: you have to think like an owl to find an owl!

❋ Farmlands. There is a variety of owls known as barn owls, which live primarily in barns and, more generally, around farm areas. If you think about it, this really makes good sense because farms are usually loaded with small mammals of one kind or another. This is ideal prey for our feathered friends!

Also, it's very important to remember that you should always be with an adult that you trust when you go on your owl safari. And if you go on someone else's property, make sure you have permission to do so. You can get into a lot of trouble for trespassing.

What Do I Do?

Barn owls are so-named because they live in and around barns—good information to have on your owl safari.

❋ Have patience. This is very important because owls can be difficult to spot (remember—they don't want to be seen). They blend in amazingly well with their surroundings and usually don't show themselves until they're ready to swoop down and grab something. They're not like many other birds that fly around all the time, landing here and there. Owls are very stationary creatures for the most part, so you may find yourself waiting awhile before you see one.

❋ Keep still and quiet. Owls are fairly tolerant of people—but not people who can't keep still! The advantage of bringing a folding chair is that you can sit and be comfortable while you're waiting.

Areas that have a lot of rodents will attract owls.

If you make a lot of noise or move around a lot, you'll not only distract the owls but also scare off their prey. This will not help you on your safari.

❋ Listen. Owls don't make a lot of noise, even when they're flying. But they do hoot and make other vocalizations, or sounds. If you stay quiet, you just might be able to hear some of them. When you do, you'll be better able to find the exact location

Safari Tip
Any night is a good night to go on an owl safari, but the best nights are when there's a full moon. This isn't to help the owls—it's to help you. Some owl enthusiasts bring along a flashlight on their safaris, but this is risky because a beam of light can easily scare off both owls and the animals they hunt. So do yourself a favor and go on your own safari when there's plenty of moonlight.

where an owl is sitting. You may have to move to get closer, which is fine, but try to do this as quietly as possible. Sometimes a hoot or a screech might be your only chance of locating an owl because, otherwise, their camouflage will make them nearly impossible to see.

❋ Watch. An owl's biggest advantage over its prey is its ability to launch a surprise attack. That means it will appear very suddenly, fly low, grab its prey, and then fly off, all in a matter of seconds. Since this happens so quickly, you really need to be alert at all times. It is very easy to miss an owl attack if you're distracted even briefly.

❋ Keep your camera ready at all times. You can capture an owl on film, but you need to be both quick and lucky. Since you'll need to take shots at night, you'll also need to use your flash. One or two quick shots of an owl in flight shouldn't distract it all that much. Just be careful not to create a kind of strobe effect, that is, a lot of flashing light. That may very well confuse and frighten an owl.

❋ Keep notes in your notebook. When you do see an owl, write down any information you feel is important. What did it look like? How big was it? Where were you when you saw it? What time did you see it? Was it the same time as the night before? After you gather enough data, you might begin to see patterns emerge that'll help you with future safaris.

❋ When you return home, download any pictures you took, and show them to your friends and family. You could also write a more formal journal, using both the pictures you took and the notes you made. You could keep an ongoing record of your owl safaris from year to year.

It's also worth noting that owls can be found, seen, and enjoyed during daylight hours, too. Many of them can be seen sleeping on branches, in tree holes, or along the edges of buildings. But remember that there won't be much to see other than the owl itself. Most owl species are inactive during the day and usually sleep. On the other hand, daylight observations enable you to not only more easily locate their habitat but also take much better photos.

Always bring along a camera on your safari—if you do see an owl or two, you'll want to capture the memory forever.

THREE
A Guide to Owls

There are about three dozen owl species in North America. All roughly have the same basic body shape and design. Identifying which ones are in your area can be challenging, but not impossible. Following the information below should help you with this.

Look over the notes you took while you were in the field along with those pictures you took (if you were lucky enough to get any). Now, try to answer the following questions:

* What was the owl's "base" color (the most prominent color)? Did it have any markings or colors beyond that? If so, what were they? How would you describe them?

* Did it have large and obvious ears, or was the head more rounded (almost as if there were no ears at all)?

* What color were the eyes? Some owls have very striking eye coloration, such as yellow or orange.

* Was there a colored ring around the facial disc?

* Did the owl make any noises? If so, how would you describe them?

Now, go to the next page and see if any of the owls in the photos match up with the characteristics that you noted in your answers. And remember that you should use other information such as your location (town, state, country) and the exact habitat in which you saw them to provide the final pieces of your puzzle. Try doing a little research on the Internet, too. Further resources are also provided for you in this book, in the Find Out More section.

Long-eared Owl

Short-eared Owl

Great Horned Owl

Elf Owl

Eastern Screech Owl

Spotted Owl

FOUR

Try This! Projects You Can Do

You might not be a professional **ornithologist** (someone who studies birds for a living), but that doesn't mean you can't do things to help owls live a better life. The following are a few relatively easy projects that will give you a more hands-on approach to your enthusiasm for owls.

Build a Nesting Box

Owls are never more in need of a good place to hide as when they lay their eggs and then take care of their young. You can help with this by building a simple nesting box and then setting it in an ideal location. You'll need an adult's help since some pieces of wood will have to be cut. You'll want a rectangular box with the top and bottom about 8 inches (20 cm) square and the sides about 16 to 18 inches (40 to 46 cm) in length. It is important to note that the front should be higher than the back, which means the top piece (the roof) will slant downward. This is so rainwater will run off the box rather than puddle and rot the wood. Make a hole in the front (near the top) about 4 to 5 inches (10 to 13 cm) in diameter so the owl can get in and out. Also, put a few small holes through the bottom for drainage in case any water does get inside. You can also place wood shavings or twigs at the bottom. The owl will probably add some things as well. Place the box in a tree where there's plenty of leaf cover, so the owl feels hidden. Make sure the box is well attached, as you don't want it falling out. If you're lucky, a mother owl will find the box and build her nest inside.

If you build a nesting box for owls, make sure you place it high enough in a tree for the owls to feel safe and comfortable.

Cleanup Time

Like any other living creature, owls need a clean **environment** in order to thrive. Unfortunately, we live in a world where natural habitats are suffering more and more from the presence of humans. When an owl's home range becomes littered with trash, it has a devastating effect on all the animals that live there. If one animal suffers, all the others in the natural cycle will suffer as well. And if an owl feels that it cannot reliably

Owl First Aid

During one of your owl safaris, you might come across an owl that appears to be sick. An owl that is on the ground, for example, may have some kind of illness or even an injury to its wings. In such cases, you may be tempted to get close to the owl or even touch it. Don't do this! An adult should be with you. Ask that person to try to gently trap the owl in a box or similar cage, and bring it to a safe place. This means placing the owl in a garage, barn, or other area outside of your home. That way you can keep it temporarily in a place where it will be safe from predators. Then, immediately call your local animal control organization (most towns have these), zoo, or your police department. An owl that is sick or injured can be very dangerous, no matter how good your intentions are. Owls are not used to being close to humans and might confuse your wanting to help as an attack. In that case, it may try to defend itself. Remember—that beak and those claws are very sharp.

find prey every night, it will move to a different location rather than risk starvation. This will make your future safaris much less rewarding. If you know of an area where owls live, you can help prevent this by routinely checking to see that it is free of waste products. Old soda cans or bottles, plastic bags or wrappers, and cigarette butts are all things that pose a serious threat. Take the time to go out with a trash bag and a pair of gloves and do a little tidying up. As with so many other activities mentioned in this book, you should bring an adult along in case you come across broken glass, rusty nails, or any number of other dangerous items. By making an effort to care for such an environment, you will be performing a great service to the creatures that live there. Too bad they can't return the favor by coming to your house and cleaning your room!

Find-the-Prey Game

You'll need a friend or two to help you with this one. And don't forget a flashlight. Everyone goes into the backyard (if you don't have one, you can try doing this inside). One person is chosen as the "owl" and the others are the "prey." The prey animals hide while the owl tries to find them using nothing but sound. The prey animals should make some noise, but not too much. The owl has to then remain completely quiet and try to locate the prey by listening. When the owl thinks it knows where its prey is hiding, it "hits" the prey with a quick, single flash of the flashlight. If the owl misses, it loses a point (or the prey scores a point). If the owl hits the prey, it scores a point. The players should take turns being the owl and the prey, and each "hunting session" should have a time limit (say, 5 minutes). When everyone has had a turn playing the owl, the person with the most points is the winner.

Trek Talk

Sometimes owls can be coaxed into view by people who know how to imitate their calls. Once you've learned which species live in your area, you can access the Internet and learn about the sounds they make. It will probably take time and practice to get them just right, but the results can be very rewarding. There are few things more exciting than making an "owl call" into a dark night and hearing a real owl call back to you! Even if this doesn't happen, learning how to make owl sounds at home can be a lot of fun.

Glossary

Aves	a class of animals that includes all birds
camouflage	the color of an animal that helps it blend in with its surroundings
carnivore	an animal that eats the meat of other animals
characteristic	a specific trait or quality that an animal has, such as tan fur or brown eyes
environment	the general type of place where an animal lives, such as a forest, swamp, or desert
facial disc	a roundish arrangement of feathers on an owl's face that helps it capture and channel sounds to its ears
habitat	place where an animal lives, such as a burrow, cave, or shoreline
invertebrate	an animal that does not have a backbone, or vertebrae
mammal	any warm-blooded animal belonging to the class known as Mammalia. Mammals are covered in hair or fur, and nurse their babies on mother's milk.
nocturnal	active during the night
ornithologist	someone who studies birds
predator	an animal that hunts other animals
prey	any animal that is hunted by another animal
species	one particular type of animal
talon	a claw, particularly that of a bird of prey
territorial	an animal that is protective of the area in which it lives
vertebrae	a group of bones that make up the spinal column

Find Out More

Books

Gregory, Josh. *Owls*. New York: Scholastic Publishing, 2013.
Owen, Ruth. *Snowy Owls*. New York: Windmill Books, 2013.
Phillips, Dee. *Spotted Owl*. New York: Bearport Publishing, 2013.

Websites

Science Kids / Fun Owl Facts

sciencekids.co.nz/sciencefacts/animals/owl.html
Good selection of "fast facts" covering all the owl basics, written at a level easy for youngsters to understand.

The Great Horned Owl (San Diego Zoo)

kids.sandiegozoo.org/animals/birds/great-horned-owl-1
This page is dedicated to the Great Horned Owl (a common North American species) with facts, activities, and color photos.

Facts About Owls (Find Fast)

findfast.org/facts-about-owls.htm
Learn more facts about owls. This "Find Fast" page also has color photos and links to further websites.

Index

Page numbers in **boldface** are illustrations.

Aves, 5

barn owl, **16**
"base" color, 5, 21

camouflage, **5**, 5, 18
carnivore, 11
characteristic, 6, 21-22
cycle of life, 11-12

eastern screech owl, **23**
elf owl, **23**
environment, 25, 27

facial disc, 7, **8**, 21
feathers, 7-8

great horned owl, **23**

habitat, 9-10, 15-16
hunt, 7-8, 11, **11**, 18-19

invertebrate, 11

lifespan, 12
long eared owl, **22**

mammal, 11
mating, 11-12

nesting box, 24-25, **25**
nocturnal, 10

ornithologist, 24
owl
    ears, 7, 21
    eyes, **6**, 6-7, 21
    helping an, 24-27, **26**
    size, 5
    sounds, 8-9, 18, 28

predator, 5
prey, 5, 7-8, 11, 16, **17**, 18

species, 7, 12, 20, 21
spotted owl, **23**

talon, 8, **9**
territorial, 9, 12

vertebrae, 6

About the Author

WIL MARA is an award-winning author of more than 140 books. He began his writing career with several titles about herpetology, the study of reptiles and amphibians. He has since branched out into other subject areas and continued to write educational books for children. To find out more about Mara and his work, you can visit his website at www.wilmara.com.